NATURE NOTES

NATURE NOTES

Peter Brookes

LITTLE, BROWN AND COMPANY

A *Little, Brown* Book

These 'Nature Notes' cartoons first published in *The Times* between February 1996 and June 1997
First published in this collection in Great Britain in 1997 by Little, Brown and Company

Copyright © 1997 by Peter Brookes and Times Newspapers, Ltd

ISBN: 0 316 64153 7

Typeset by M Rules in Bembo
Printed and bound in Great Britain by Butler & Tanner Ltd, Frome and London

Little, Brown and Company (UK)
Brettenham House
Lancaster Place
London WC2E 7EN

For Angela, Benjamin and William

John Major, having appointed Sir Richard Scott to report on the arms-to-Iraq scandal, then has to defend ministers William Waldegrave and Sir Nicholas Lyell against severe criticism in Scott's findings.

Divorce negotiations between lawyers acting for the Prince and Princess of Wales become increasingly acrimonious.

Michael Heseltine admits to late payments to small businesses when he was making his fortune. He is also known to have arranged vast office space for himself in 10a Downing Street as Deputy Prime Minister.

The government acknowledges for the first time that 'mad cow' disease can be transmitted to people. John Gummer, when he was Minister for Agriculture, famously and publicly fed his daughter Cordelia a hamburger in order to demonstrate beef's 'safety'.

NATURE NOTES

Peter Brookes
23 iii 96

EC Council Directive (96/84/B)
THIS CAN
SERIOUSLY DAMAGE
YOUR HEALTH

Suffolk Shorthorn (*Bovine gum-gum*).
Maddening creature with a thick hide which chooses
to feed its young in public. Will probably be slaughtered
with the whole herd at a General Election.

Douglas Hogg, Minister for Agriculture, fails to get the British beef ban lifted at the emergency meeting of European Union farm ministers in Luxembourg.

Shimon Peres attacks Hezbollah bases in Lebanon; Major's majority is cut to one after the Staffordshire South-East by-election; and Boris Yeltsin continues to face resistance from the Chechen guerrillas.

NATURE NOTES

Threatened species of the world

Dove
(Peres israelis)
Is having to adapt in
a hostile environment.
Now hawkish.

Greytit
(Majorus reductus)
Last sighting in
S.E. Staffs. Could
be gone by next
spring.

Two-headed Eagle
(Yeltsina vodka)
Erratic flight path.
Prone to seeing double.

20 iv 96

Peter Brookes

The Conservative party loses hundreds of council seats across England. Even Basildon, symbol of 1980s Thatcherism, falls to Labour. The Tory Chairman Brian Mawhinney declares it to be an 'improvement' on the previous year.

F. W. de Klerk's National Party decides to withdraw from Nelson Mandela's Government of National Unity in South Africa.

NATURE NOTES

White-billed Oxpecker (*de Klerkus sudafricanus*).
Symbiotic with the black rhinoceros, this bird
feeds on the back of the giant pachyderm. Flies from
its host as soon as it spots danger.

Peter Brookes 11·V·96

The Lord Chief Justice, Lord Taylor, along with other Law Lords, savagely attacks Michael Howard's White Paper on sentencing.

President Clinton's Whitewater partners are found guilty of numerous conspiracy and fraud charges in Little Rock, Arkansas.

Ian Paisley, leader of the Democratic Unionists, declares his opposition to US Senator George Mitchell chairing all-party talks on Northern Ireland.

Baroness Thatcher ostentatiously donates money to Bill Cash's anti-federalist European Foundation, and is rebuked by an angry John Major. A bat, thought to have come from France to Newhaven, is confirmed to be carrying the rabies virus.

Tony Blair proposes to hold a referendum on a Scottish parliament, thereby sharply shifting Labour's position on devolution.

NATURE NOTES

Scottish U-Tern
(Electus forgodsake)

By flexing its backbone, this bird can adopt an uncomfortable *refer-endum* position.

29 vi 96

Peter Brookes

In the Russian election, ailing President Yeltsin relies heavily on the questionable support of his new National Security Advisor, General Alexsandr Lebed, who opposed him in the first round.

NATURE NOTES

Muscovy Lame Duck
(Invodka invicta)

Suffers from a weak constitution and has to be propped up.
Makes its own *Lebed* and must now lie on it.

David Trimble, leader of the Ulster Unionists, is prominent in the protest against the Royal Ulster Constabulary's decision to re-route the Orange Order march away from a Catholic area at Drumcree.

NATURE NOTES

Peter Brookes
13 vii 96

Fig. 1
Fully mature

Fig. 2
Development

Orange Tip Butterfly
(*Trimbleris triumphalus*)

Flutters uneasily between the *environs* of Westminster and a harsh constituency habitat. March breeder.

Sir Edward Heath celebrates his eightieth birthday. Is Baroness Thatcher invited to the party?

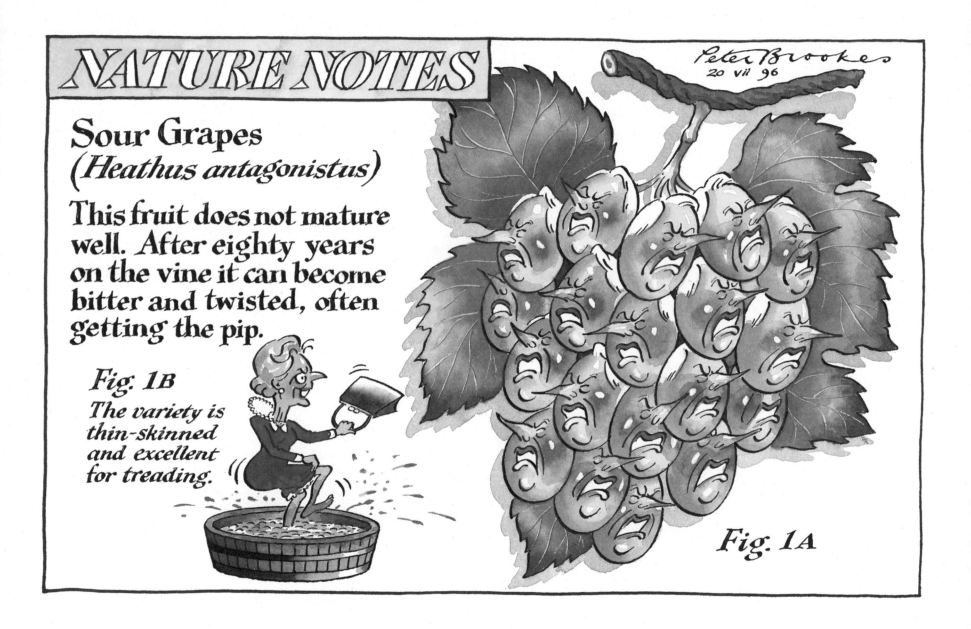

NATURE NOTES

Peter Brookes
20 vii 96

Sour Grapes
(*Heathus antagonistus*)

This fruit does not mature well. After eighty years on the vine it can become bitter and twisted, often getting the pip.

Fig. 1B
The variety is thin-skinned and excellent for treading.

Fig. 1A

Clare Short is demoted from her position as Shadow Cabinet Transport spokesperson to Overseas Development after a series of gaffes (on legalising cannabis, on Harriet Harman's decision to send her son to a selective school and on Labour's tax plans), culminating in walking out of a television interview after she had been challenged over the Tube strikes.

Home Secretary Michael Howard suspends the blundered early release of hundreds of prisoners and is supported by the courts.

NATURE NOTES

Peter Brookes
31 viii 96

Howard's Carp (*Dontblamemeus itsnotmyfaultus*)
Impossible to keep on the hook. Has very sharp teeth and
a slippery body. Oleaginous.

The US hits Iraq with twenty-seven Cruise missiles to prevent Saddam attacking his neighbours (and American interests) in Operation Desert Strike. It does no harm to the Democrats' re-election bid – nor to Saddam Hussein.

Fig. 1

Flesh Fly (*Saddamus pestilensis*)
Small flesh-eating parasite with a vicious bite. Dictatorial by habit but can be helpful to Democrats. Ignores no-fly zones.

Humphrey Carpenter's biography of Robert Runcie makes use of taped interviews with the ex-Primate, who thought his views, particularly regarding the royal marriage and Prince Charles's future as king, were off the record.

45

NATURE NOTES

Canterbury Lamb (*Runcius Ineverthoughtyou'dusethis*)
Woolly breed which can stray from a position of trust. Will
bleat incessantly when prompted.

14 ix 96
Peter Brookes

The Tory party is again riven by splits after John Redwood and other leading Eurosceptics turn on the party grandees who have warned John Major that he must keep open the option of joining a single currency.

The Labour Party looks forward to its conference in Blackpool, but John Prescott warns Tony Blair not to modernise too fast as he risks 'hitting the buffers'.

NATURE NOTES

Peter Brookes
28 ix 96

Fig. 1
Cooker

Fig. 2
Blossom

Prescottia vulgaris

Blairum superiore

Conference Pears (*Newlabora insipidis*)
Acidic yet sweet, rough-skinned yet cultured, this fruit (if served with enough syrup) is palatable to all tastes.

Chancellor Kenneth Clarke is promised a rough ride at the forthcoming
Conservative party conference in Bournemouth because of his Europhile position.

NATURE NOTES

Peter Brookes
5 X 96

Large Pink (*Currencis singularis*)

Much fancied for sausage meat at the Bournemouth Show, but is proving a hardy swine and could save its bacon.

The Tory conference is brought to a rousing finale by John Major after it was expected to be split further by differences over Europe. For the moment, unity reigns.

NATURE NOTES

Brussels Sprouts
(*Unitatus youmustbekiddingus*)

Held together by a fragile, single stem, this brassica is usually served in a stew, accompanied by a right old pickle. Runs to seed in May.

Fig.1
Cooking method:
Keep lid firmly on
or contents will soon
boil over.

Peter Brookes 12 x 96

Sir James Goldsmith proposes a referendum on withdrawal from the European Union and seeks to oppose all Europhile candidates in the General Election.

NATURE NOTES

Fig. 1 Position of utmost gravity

French Goldsmith Delicious *(Major's endum referendum)*
This import has gained prominence by aggressive, expensive marketing. Leaves a sour taste in many MP's mouths.

Peter Brookes 19 X 96

John Major performs a U-turn on crime, by accepting Tony Blair's offer of assistance with piloting through measures to tackle stalkers and child-sex offenders.

Gillian Shephard's initiative to bring back corporal punishment is not endorsed by John Major.

Mohamed al-Fayed, owner of Harrods, wins a crucial battle in his long-running fight for British citizenship when the Court of Appeal quashes the government's refusal to grant it.

NATURE NOTES

Peter Brookes
16 XI 96

CONSERVATIVE PARTY

FAYEDO

British Bulldog *(Giveus apassportus)*
Of mixed pedigree, it is pugnacious and tenacious. Available
for cash from Harrods pet department, no questions asked.

The government is forced to concede an EMU debate in the Commons by Eurosceptics angered by John Major's equivocal stance on Europe.

No surprises in a prudent Budget as all details are leaked to the *Daily Mirror*.

Fig.1 Serving suggestion

Leaks (*Budgetis bodgetis*)

Treasury recipes include an embarrassing stew of neutral and bland flavours. Try with *confit* of mole for added piquancy.

The Chancellor threatens his Prime Minister, who has reportedly wobbled on the sacrosanct 'wait-and-see' policy on a single European currency. Major later retracts.

Labour wipes out the government's majority of one in the Commons by decisively winning the Barnsley East by-election, with more than 77 per cent of the vote.

NATURE NOTES

Peter Brookes
14 xii 96

Scrag End of Lamb
After the Barnsley chop, not much remains of these chumps.
Try kebabbed with fresh vegetables. New Labour, new potatoes.

Christmas card from *The Times*, December 1996.

NATURE NOTES

Christmas Turkeys (*Quattuorhoræ gasmarktres*)
These birds emit an increasingly shrill "gobbledegook" whilst being prepared for an election roasting. Not trussworthy.

Tony Blair and Jack Straw endorse 'zero tolerance' towards aggressive begging in an interview in the *Big Issue*. John Major accuses them of hypocritically stealing Tory measures.

NATURE NOTES

Fig: 1

Maggiepies
(*Tendencia thatcheritis*)

These thieving *corvidæ* are attracted by the glittering property of others. Displaying a pronounced right wing bias, they fly in ever-decreasing circles, eventually disappearing up their own *manifesto*.

John Major continues to equivocate over the single currency issue.

NATURE NOTES

Peter Brookes
18 i 97

Hedgerhog *(Europa dithera)*
If this sad creature persists in its middle-of-the-road position it can expect to be kohled in large numbers.

Michael Portillo, Defence Secretary, announces a replacement for the Royal Yacht *Britannia* and an expansion of the school cadet force in a blatant show of electioneering.

NATURE NOTES

Keep well away from brussels and frankfurters

Cadet size

Spanish Onion *(Portillista hubrista)*
Pungently flavoured import, lately introduced to *Britannia*. Gets up noses and is enough to make strong men weep.

Sir George Gardiner is de-selected by his Reigate Conservative Association after publishing criticism of John Major as Kenneth Clarke's ventriloquist dummy.

Labour prepares to govern.

Parliament prepares a censure motion on Douglas Hogg's handling of the BSE crisis; Stephen Dorrell's gaffe on Scottish devolution has him sidelined; and John Major continues to be John Major.

Chancellor Kenneth Clarke is isolated after Malcolm Rifkind, the Foreign Secretary, breaks the Cabinet truce on Europe and declares the government to be 'hostile' to a single European currency.

Lord McAlpine attacks John Major (and most of the Cabinet) in his memoirs; Lord Tebbit savages Michael Heseltine in the *Spectator*.

NATURE NOTES

Skunk
(*McAlpinus memoirus*)
Lethal marauder which
can cause a dreadful stink.

Polecat (*Chingfordus stranglerus*)
Semi-housetrained, it emerges from hibernation
to create mayhem in the coop.

Douglas Hogg and Michael Forsyth openly row over a new food–hygiene scare (*E.coli*, sourced to bad practice in abattoirs); after the recent massive defeat in the Wirral South by-election the Tories continue to bicker; John Redwood wonders who is leading the election campaign.

The Tories slump in the polls as their General Election campaign is launched. King, their lachrymose poster lion, is supposed to portray patriotic aggression but is described by his trainer as a 'non-roaring wimp'.

Sleaze allegations continue to overshadow the Tory election campaign as transcript evidence from the Downey investigation into the cash-for-questions scandal is published.

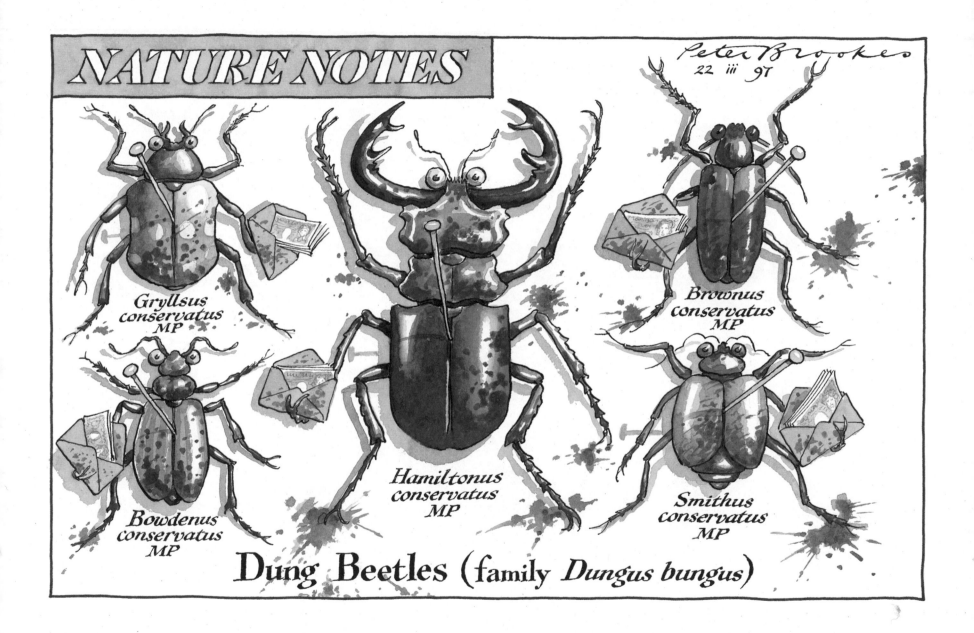

The Liberal Democrats look set to be squeezed by Labour in the election. (In fact, because of tactical voting to kick out the Tories, they do much better than expected.)

NATURE NOTES

N.B. *The fruit is bitter if not on the moral high ground.*

Lemon (*Liberalis nohopers*)

Flourishes in the warmth of the West Country but shows a patchy growth elsewhere. Familiar varieties include 'Action Man', 'Holier-than-thou' and 'Pantsdown'. Should ripen for squeezing by May.

Fig. 1

A juicy constituency

Peter Brookes 12 iv 97

Can the Labour Party of Margaret Beckett *et al* be a moderate party?

NATURE NOTES

Painted Lady
(*Becketta oldlabora*)

Fig.1 Upperside

Fig.2 Underside

It uses its top profile to blend in with new surroundings and to disguise the true colouring beneath. Flutters to deceive.

Peter Brookes 26 iv 97

Labour wins the General Election on 1 May 1997 with an overall majority of 179.

Following their crushing election defeat the six candidates for the leadership of the Conservative party declare themselves.

Ann Widdecombe, the former Prisons Minister, is determined to wreck ex-Home Secretary Michael Howard's leadership chances by revealing the details behind his sacking of the prisons director Derek Lewis.

NATURE NOTES

Fig. 1

Black Widowcombe Spider
(Somethingus ofthenightus)

Venomous and venge-
ful, its bite induces
paralysis. The male
is then killed and
eaten by sucking in
as liquid. (Just
dessert)

17 V 97

Peter Brookes

After the French elections, the right-wing President Jacques Chirac has to accept working with his new socialist Prime Minister, Lionel Jospin.

William Hague (aged 36¾) becomes the surprise front-swimmer in a three-fish race for the Tory leadership.

NATURE NOTES

Baby Octopus (*Hagueis vagueis*)

Protected and surrounded by a surprisingly large number of suckers. Propels itself rapidly through the shallows, rising without trace. Adapts its colouring to changing circumstances. Invertebrate.

Rows of suckers

Fig.1 An opaque squirt confounds its enemies

Peter Brookes 14 vi 97

After John Redwood's elimination, Hague silences his remaining opponent.

Former Defence Procurement minister Jonathan Aitken withdraws his libel action against the *Guardian* and Granada TV after evidence is revealed that he lied to the High Court.

NATURE NOTES

Liar-bird
(Aitkenus dissemblus)

The male develops a unique tail that features in its frequent courtship dances. It nests exclusively in Parisian hotel buildings and migrates to shady regions in Saudi. Plunges from a great height.

Fig. 1 The parent behaves atrociously towards its young.

Fig. 2

28 vi 97
Peter Brookes